Networking - Expand your network professional

Yves Guéchi

Published by Yves Guéchi, 2024.

While every precaution has been taken in the preparation of this book, the publisher assumes no responsibility for errors or omissions, or for damages resulting from the use of the information contained herein.

NETWORKING - EXPAND YOUR NETWORK PROFESSIONAL

First edition. February 22, 2024.

ISBN: 979-8224265572

Written by Yves Guéchi.

Table of Contents

Networking

Expand your network

professional

Yves Guéchi

Pedagogical Engineer

Check your work

"Networking is not about collecting contacts, it's the art of cultivating meaningful and lasting relationships." – Ivan Misner

According to the theory of 6 degrees of separation established in 1929 by a Hungarian researcher, Frigyes Karinthy, you are connected to anyone in the world by a maximum of 5 individuals. That's right: according to this research, you're only 5 people away from your favorite star, celebrity, or athlete you admire!

What if you could use this proximity to anyone in the world to create more **opportunities** for yourself? Why not seek out a relationship with business leaders in your industry? With recognized experts? With other enthusiasts like you to exchange information? What if you took advantage of the connections you will develop to learn new **skills,** progress in your career, **collaborate** on new projects?

Our world is accelerating, distances are getting shorter, social networks are developing and the use of mobile applications allows us to always be connected and available. Properly exploited, these are real **opportunities,** which you will learn to cultivate here.

In this course, you'll learn about everything networking has to offer. You'll learn how to grow your **network, how to use** social media **to approach the right people strategically, and how to maintain that network over time.**

*Ready to network? To meet new people? To discover a new **strategy** to create new opportunities for yourself? Then you've come to the right place! See you in the first chapter, to start this adventure together!*

Part 1 - Think about your networking strategy
Chapter I

———

Integrate the basics of the network

You've probably heard expressions like:

"It's not about what you know, it's about who you know."

"Those who travel alone go fast, those who travel with a companion go far."

"There's the lawyer who knows the law, and the one who knows the judge."

These expressions emphasize, with irony or sometimes humor, the importance of having a **strong network** to achieve one's goals.

In English, a quote that is widely circulated even goes so far as to say "If you are not networking, you are NOT working".

Before looking at how to network and maintain your network, let's take a look at the notion of **networking** and especially the benefits you can expect by implementing your **network strategy**.

What is networking?

NETWORKING IS SIMPLY the deliberate and thoughtful action of building a network of people related to your sectors of activity or your passions, with whom you will be able to **exchange** to create **professional opportunities**.

We're talking about something very simple, and one that you're probably already doing: building solid **human relationships**. What's going to change is the thoughtful, strategic, and systematic approach that you're going to take and that we'll detail throughout this course.

> *Whether it's via social networks and the internet, or via more traditional "offline" techniques, it's about creating a strong **relational bond** that you can use in one way or another to achieve your goals.*

Today, whatever your professional ambitions, having a network on which you can rely is **essential**. In some positions, it is one of the main recruitment criteria, as it is a strong differentiator between candidates.

> For certain commercial functions or editorial or journalistic functions, for example, being able to prove that you know the right people is often a decisive element.

Let's take a closer look at the benefits you'll get from a **structured** and **applied networking approach**.

Why network?

WHETHER YOU ARE LOOKING for a job, an entrepreneur or a business creator, a student, a professional retraining or a freelancer, networking is for everyone.

Like personal branding, it should help you move forward in your **professional project**. Everyone is therefore concerned, regardless of age, seniority, geography or sector of activity. But for what, exactly?

The Power of Recommendation

A FEW MONTHS AGO, I was contacted by a business school who wanted to know if I could intervene with their students. I hadn't applied; It was someone in my network, with whom I had made a presentation a few weeks earlier, who **recommended** me to this pedagogical director whom she knows personally. This led to a new opportunity.

Similarly, a few years ago, my employer was looking for an intern. I simply recommended a student I had befriended when I was teaching.

> *Many companies use **co-optation**. They ask their employees to refer them for open positions, with a reward at stake.*

Having the **right connections** and being identified by your network as a good candidate opens the doors to these opportunities, and many others, that are not even published.

Finally, you probably regularly see people on social networks, and especially on LinkedIn, who call on their network to share their CV or to help them get in touch with recruiters.

> *Having a solid and mobilized network allows you to **gain visibility**, generate engagement and why not land a new job.*

Learn new skills

YOUR NETWORK CAN ALSO help you learn. Whether it's by sharing online courses that have been followed by acquaintances who have a similar profile to yours, by recommending courses or events that will allow you to acquire **new skills**, your network is the perfect place to **learn** from your contacts.

You're likely to have people with a wide range of skills in your network.

Learn through your network!

THROUGH SHARING AND discussions with all these people, you will naturally enrich your own and learn in the long term **useful skills** for the development of your career, or for a personal interest. This is an asset that is often little perceived by a good network.

Keep up to date with the latest news in your industry

BY BEING CONNECTED to the right people, such as thought leaders or leaders in your industry, you are almost certain not to miss any key news. Always informed and up-to-date with the **latest news**, you become an essential asset to your company, which can rely on your knowledge.

Well **informed**, you also become a strategic partner for your customers and increase your credibility and even your creativity, because you are aware of the latest trends.

*The more news **you receive from your network, the more you participate in the** events **they organize, the more you feed off different experiences and content to get** new ideas **and see your business from a different perspective.***

Increase your influence and visibility

THANKS TO YOUR NETWORK, you are already better informed and more credible. But even better, it will also allow you **to be more visible**, because it will be able to reshare your content or publications.

Virality is one of the fundamental principles of social media, and if you have built a quality network, you can rely on it to interact with your content and make it more visible.

Your articles or videos can be shared and viewed hundreds or even thousands of times just because your nearest network will have shared it with their network, who will have shared it with their network, etc., organically amplifying your visibility.

But for this to happen, your contacts must see you as a **credible person**, and they must want, for personal reasons, to give you this visibility. Hence the importance, in this situation, of a well-worked and maintained network.

But while the benefits are numerous, networking is not necessarily as easy as it seems. Let's take a look at the limitations you may face.

What are the obstacles you may encounter?

A process that can seem intimidating

SINCE WE'RE TALKING about human relationships, networking obviously means meeting others. Whether it's behind a computer or during a face-to-face event, building a network requires talking to strangers and creating an interesting discussion with them. This can be scary, especially for the shyest! You have to dare to reach out to other people, and find relevant topics to discuss. That's a lot!

> *If you're worried about stepping out of your comfort zone, don't hesitate to ask people you know well to help you with this, especially at the beginning, before it becomes automatic.*

For example, ask a mutual contact to connect you on LinkedIn (we'll see how in detail) or go to events with a friend or colleague.

You'll be more comfortable, more natural, and therefore able to connect with the right people more easily.

A process that takes time

A QUOTE THAT YOU WILL often find on the internet says it very clearly:

> "Networking isn't hunting, it's breeding."

Don't expect to see the effects of your networking strategy in the first few days or weeks. **It will take time**, sometimes several months or even years, for your strategy to really pay off. And that's normal, the confidence needed to entrust a mission or a job is not acquired in a message and two articles shared on social networks.

*So be **patient, structured** and **tenacious**. What you build today will help you tomorrow! Above all, don't cut corners and think long-term!*

A sometimes awkward approach

WHAT CAN ALSO SLOW you down in your approach is the impression that you are in a self-serving approach, that it is not sincere and that you are taking advantage of others. It's **only natural** to feel that way.

*Indeed, in this process, you have many **objectives** in mind and your network must be able to help you achieve them.*

Nevertheless, be **sincere** and **genuine**. As long as you bring value to your network, that you share, that you exchange, then you are not in a one-way relationship, and you have no qualms to have.

*Networking is a two-way process: you **take** advice, contacts, opportunities from your contacts, etc., but you will also **bring** them a lot, making your requests **totally legitimate**. And they will gladly do so... in the same way that you yourself will gladly help them!*

As Reid Hoffman, founder of PayPal and LinkedIn and an investor in many start-ups, puts it:

"Your network consists of people who want to help you and whom you want to help, and that's powerful."

It's not a mercantile move, so don't be afraid to get in the way. Instead, be **open** and **curious** so that this exchange is as beneficial as possible to both parties.

That's what this course is for: giving you the keys to be able to benefit from all the benefits of networking without feeling any limits or constraints. And as you can see, these benefits are huge professionally.

Take your time, be **authentic and** strategic, **listen to your network, and learn to ask at the right time to succeed.**

In short

- Networking means building a network of people linked to your sectors of activity or passions, to exchange and create professional opportunities.

- Networking is essential to create opportunities, exchange, learn new skills, and keep up to date with the latest news in your sector.

- Are you shy, do you think you're running out of time or are you afraid that people will think you're interested in it? This course is here to take your brakes off the brakes.

Chapter II

Clarify your goals

Building your network is important, as you can see. But you're probably wondering where to start.

Should you jump in right away and send **out LinkedIn invitations** ? Want to start **networking** at an event next weekend? Contacting a former classmate to tell them about a project they should be interested in? No, those are not your priorities.

In order to know which of these actions (or others) is the most suitable and important for you, you need to pause and ask yourself the right questions. And the first one, which will guide your entire networking strategy, is to understand what you want to do and what you want to **get out** of your network.

So you need to start by setting **clear goals**.

Set clear goals

IT'S A REFLEX TO WANT to find solutions right away and put them in place. You've probably already experienced it. For example, if a friend tells you that he wants to lose weight, you will immediately tell him to do sports, without **analyzing the whole problem** and other possible solutions.

It's the same for networking. If you don't know why you're doing it, you won't see all the options you can **explore, and** your approach will be laborious and ineffective.

Finally, if you don't know exactly what you want to accomplish, you'll network with people who aren't relevant, looking for **quantity** rather than **quality**. You'll be wasting valuable time that you won't invest in achieving.

Plan for the short, medium and long term

AS YOU CAN SEE, NETWORKING is a **long-term** strategy, so being able to project yourself is essential. Still, if your shorter-term goals are clear, your network can also help you make rapid progress. Define them clearly.

Short-term

YOUR PROFESSIONAL PRIORITIES for the next few weeks and months: finding an internship or a job, getting a raise, finding a partner or an investor to launch your project...

> *Note that these goals can be steps in a longer-term strategy. Breaking down an ambitious goal into **specific**, simpler tasks keeps you focused and motivated.*

To help you achieve them, you will need to have in your network mainly relatives or people linked to your sector of activity: colleagues, managers of your company, recruiters, etc.

Long-term

IT'S ABOUT YOUR LIFE ambitions more broadly, in the next 10 years and beyond. It is your **motivations, your** passions, **your** ambitions that will help you formulate them. Depending on the results of this vision, you will surely work your network very differently.

> *For example, if you want to change jobs or professional sectors, you will look to network with people with these profiles. If you want to start your own business, you'll want to look for profiles similar to the one you'd like to have in the long run.*

Medium term

THESE ARE ALL THE INTERMEDIATE objectives to move from your short-term vision to the long-term one, all the **steps** you will go through and which will allow you to **confirm** or **reorient** your professional project.

In terms of networking, these can be the intermediary contacts that you will go through to contact people who can help you in a longer-term project.

> *For example, if you would like to benefit from **the advice** of a very large business leader to set up your own, your intermediate objectives could be to meet other people in the company and its **circle of influence** so that this meeting is possible afterwards.*

For example, setting up your tech start-up is a long-term goal that will require you to go through a number **of steps**, in the short or medium term.

Finding THE right idea, testing it with your network, resigning from your current position,

finding partners to accompany you in this adventure will be short-term objectives that will lead you to this start-up.

In the medium term, you will have to draw up a business plan, find investors, create your first prototypes, etc. While your primary goal is long-term, you will still have to go through a number of steps, in the short or medium term.

To help you build your goals, don't hesitate to use the **SMART method** (set yourself Specific, Measurable, Achievable, Realistic and Time-Bound goals).

Examples of SMART goals applied to your networking strategy:

- Get in touch with a start-up founder in the banking sector before the end of the month

- Identify 3 people who can connect me with someone from Company X before the end of the week

- Reach 500 qualified LinkedIn relationships within 6 months

Define your personas

ONCE YOU'VE CLARIFIED these goals, you'll be able to define exactly who your network needs to have to achieve them. Take into account all possible dimensions to try to refine the **typical portrait** of people who could have an impact in achieving your goals.

*Like an investigator, try to build a **composite portrait** of these people, so you will know more easily where and how to look for them.*

Geography

DOES YOUR PROJECT HAVE an international dimension or is it anchored in a local territory? Depending on your answer, it will be easier for you to know where to develop your network.

Seniority

*Do you need the experience of people with high positions in the company, and perhaps more difficult to contact? Do you need a more **responsive** and **connected** network that may have less experience?*

DETERMINE THE LEVEL of experience needed to achieve your goals. Chances are, this one will be higher for your long-term goals.

Companies & Industries

ARE YOU TARGETING A specific company or industry? If that's the case, you're bound to be looking to have people in your network who can help you achieve these goals.

Posts

IF, ON THE OTHER HAND, you are targeting specific **responsibilities**, you will look to connect with people who can help you better understand these positions and who can help you network with people in similar **roles**.

If these 4 filters are the most important in general, you can of course add others, sometimes more personal: similar passions, joint studies, size of the established network, associations frequented...

When you have the opportunity to get in touch with someone, you will look at their profile through the prism of these criteria to qualify them and decide whether or not to follow through.

In order to help you use these criteria, I recommend that you create 3 to 4 "**personas**" that will serve as a decision-making tool.

*Personas are typically used in marketing to target the right consumer profiles. It is a question of defining **typical targets** by combining a certain number of criteria.*

This way, you can imagine what the ideal contacts look like to help you progress towards your goals. You create ideal fictitious people and can easily find out whether or not the contacts you have match these profiles.

Let's go back, for example, to the project of setting up your tech start-up, of which we have detailed several steps previously. Here's a persona you could create:

Denis, 40 years old, created his digital start-up 5 years ago. Settled in the Paris region. Passionate about new technologies and artificial intelligence. Works with Microsoft and Google in the US. Knows Jeff Bezos personally. Always on the go, he's mostly on his mobile or tablet...

Be as **specific** as possible, give a real identity to your ideal personas. All this information will also help you know where, how and when to contact these typical profiles.

Denis, for example, is always on the move; You will surely be able to easily contact him via social media with a very short message rather than in his company's offices or with an email that explains in detail who you are, what you do and what you expect from him.

*Whatever your goals and the personas you've established, keep in mind that while your network should help you move forward, it should also help you keep an **open mind**.*

Systematically rejecting all profiles that don't fit your personas is not a good approach. Indeed, if a good network is built around your goals, having people who bring different things to the table is a real asset.

In short

- Work in stages: set your clear short, medium, and long-term goals.

- Choose the essential people to help you get there.

- Stay open: contacts that are a priori further away from your criteria could surprise you!

Chapter III

Analyze your current networks

You know where you want to go, and you know which profiles can help you get there. Now it's time to take a look at where you're starting from in order to assess how much work you still have to do to develop the right network.

This step in the process may seem long and tedious. Nevertheless, it is essential to have a complete view of your networks and know how to move forward. Remember, this is a long-term process, so it's normal to invest time in it!

Take a tour of the networks you belong to

YOU'LL START WITH A very **macro** view of your network ecosystem. Only then will you be able to zoom in on each one.

Open a spreadsheet program (Excel or Google Sheet, your choice) and create a table with 6 columns.

- In the first one add "network", **then** "size of the network", **"knowledge of** the network" (how well do you know the people who make it up in general?), "involvement in the network" (how active are you in this network, do you invest time in it on a regular basis?), **"interest of the network in relation to your objectives**(Can you rely on the people who make up this network to reach them?) and finally **"means of contact"**. For each column, you'll use a scale between 0 and 10 to qualify the criterion (except for the last one, which is more of an action aid).

• Then go through each of your networks under the magnifying glass to try to give it **a rating** and better understand your networks of influence. Don't forget any network, be as complete as possible. This is quite a subjective job, although some networks give you access to fairly detailed statistics. Give these scores in a natural way, then proofread to refine the scores across networks.

For example, you might end up with this type of table:

Network	Waist	Knowledge	Implication	Interest VS Objectives	Contact
LinkedIn	8	6	10	8	Messages, mentions...
Facebook	5	9	4	5	Messages, mentions...
Family	2	10	9	3	Tel, e-mails
Enterprise	4	7	7	10	Phone, e-mails, appointments
Alumni	10	3	2	8	Alumni Directory

Add all the social networks on which you have an active presence, as well as all the groups to which you belong, family, neighbourhood, associations, political groupings or trade unions...

Once these scores have been established and reviewed, you can create a diagram that will allow you to have a global and simplified view of your current networks:

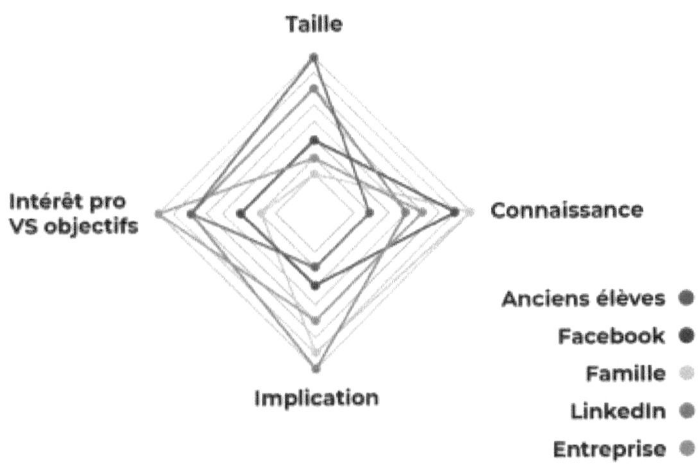

Representation of your networks

THE OBJECTIVE OF THIS first step is simply to see what the **strengths** and **weaknesses** of your different networks are, to prioritize global actions in your networking strategy.

You may have already seen this type of graph in some video games where it allows you to compare two characters to select the one that will be the most interesting. Here, it's exactly the same principle. This representation allows you to compare the different networks and see how one or the other stands out.

You can make this type of chart, known as radar, in Excel.

*Here, it is clear that the network that is the largest and most interesting professionally is the one I know the least about and where I am least involved. Starting my **networking strategy** with this network may therefore seem interesting. LinkedIn* *seems (unsurprisingly!) to be one of my strengths, I know I could capitalize on it and continue to invest time in it.*

This simple and quick visualization of your networks will allow you to have a clearer vision of your current networks and start laying the first stones of your strategy. Once this macro work is done, it's time to zoom in on some particularly relevant contacts and networks.

Zoom in on your contacts

ONCE YOU'VE GOT THIS general overview, you'll need to zoom in on the different contacts that make up your networks.

Again, this may take you some time, but it will allow you to get an accurate picture of your **current resources** and know where and how to grow your network. Throughout this work, keep your goals in mind.

If your networks are already relatively large, don't hesitate to **segment them** according to your objectives in order to zoom in where it's really relevant.

*For example, if your goal is to get into a **targeted** company, start by analyzing the people in your network who work at that company. Similarly, if your goal is a position, profession, or industry, start where that analysis makes the most sense.*

Finally, of course, start with the networks that you have identified in your previous analysis as being **the most useful** to your approach.

Here again, you will have an essentially **qualitative** approach, positioning your contacts on two axes:

- Relevance to your goals

- Person's current level of knowledge

In order to help you with this qualification, you will use your **personas**. Check to what extent the contact you are looking at fits or not with one or more of the personas you have identified so that you can again score it out of 10.

> *Don't hesitate to look at the person's profile on **social media**, their connections, their news, their activity... to help you qualify it.*

In terms of **level of knowledge**, you will also give a score (estimated of course) between 0 and 10. To be truly complete, take into account your membership in similar networks or any commonalities you may have.

For example, someone who works at your company and whom you know to be a football fan, like you, should not be considered a complete stranger, even if you have never exchanged, because relatively strong **ties** bring you together.

Once you've done that, map out the contacts to get a graph like the one below, to get a very visual overview of your network. Target this representation according to your objectives (company, sector of activity, etc.) as in this example:

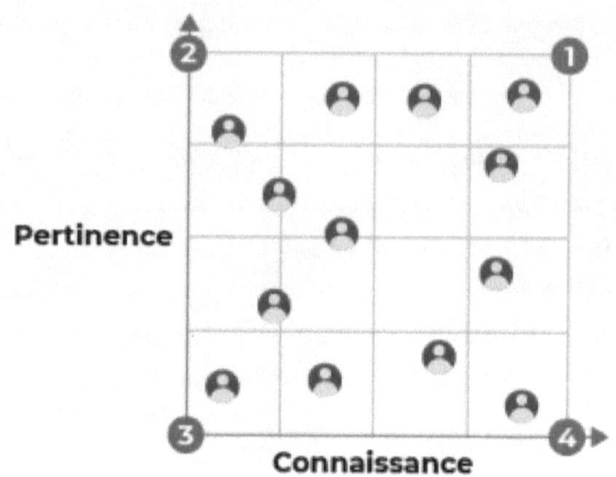

Mapping your contacts

Here you see the contacts distinguished according to the two axes of your degree of knowledge of the person, and his relevance to the objectives. This results in 4 categories of contacts.

THIS ALLOWS YOU TO quickly **visualize** the most interesting contacts and quickly decide on your strategy according to the different populations:

1. Very interesting people, whom you know well: your goal will be to make sure you are **visible** and **credible** in their eyes, and to talk to them about your projects. These people are now in the best position to help you.
2. Very relevant people, but with whom you still have a poor relationship. Your goal will be to make yourself visible to these people. First of all, you will have to **get to know them**

better, by getting information from mutual contacts or via social networks. This will give you interesting information to start a relevant discussion.

3. People you know well, but who can't have an impact on your project. Make sure that you maintain a good relationship with these people and do not hesitate to **ask for advice**, opinions... Keep in touch, you never know if they won't soon be connected to people who are very important to you!

4. People you know little or nothing about, and who are irrelevant. Be **reactive**, don't invest time and energy in developing relationships that are not very interesting for your project.

Focus on the most relevant members

NOW THAT YOU'VE PRIORITIZED your different networks as well as the different contacts in those networks, it's time to add the finishing touches to your work of analyzing your current network.

We have proceeded by progressive zoom, we are now as close as possible to the contacts you selected in the previous step. Now it's time to **fill out files** on the different people who make up your network, so that you don't forget important **details** and can expand these relationships.

> *This file should not be used as a database that you will then use in a commercial approach, don't forget that this is illegal!*

In a spreadsheet or text file, write a few lines about the people you have selected. How you got in touch, where you met, what they had in common, what information this person shared, why you think they're interesting for your project...

These quick sheets will allow you, when you interact with this person online, or if you are preparing an event where you are likely to meet them, to be more impactful and memorable, and to create strong, trusting relationships.

Over time, you won't need these cards anymore, they just serve as a reminder to get you started. They shouldn't take anything away from the naturalness of your relationships.

In short

• Take a look at your current networks, zoom in on your contacts, focus on the most relevant ones: you now have a clear vision of the strengths of your network and its enrichment to be carried out to achieve your objectives.

• These three steps will also allow you to understand in which network(s) your potential mentors are located.

Chapter IV

Rely on mentors

As you can see, networking is about **creating a link** with people who can have an impact on your personal and professional goals, at different levels. Among these people, there is one (or several, depending on the situation) who may be called upon to play a particular role. Focus on the role of "**mentor**".

What is a mentor?

TO PUT IT SIMPLY, A mentor is someone who is going to have an impact on your career and/or personal life. This can be done in a variety of ways, but it will always be someone who inspires you to help you **move forward.**

> *The mentor won't do things for you, but they will help you find the right direction, ask the right questions, and make sure you make consistent decisions to achieve the goals you've set together.*

A mentor is neither a coach nor a manager. In a relationship with a coach, there is almost only a notion of **learning**, transfer of **knowledge** and **skills**, which is too limiting. Your relationship with a mentor needs to go deeper.

In addition, when it comes to coaching, there is often a business transaction behind it. Under no circumstances should a relationship with a mentor involve financial compensation.

Your manager is also not a good mentor. While it will often guide you in your career and share **advice** and **best practices**, the hierarchical relationship will limit its possibilities.

In addition, your report will often be primarily focused on your position or company, whereas a mentor should help you see further and explore all the possibilities and opportunities.

What is the purpose of a mentor?

YOUR MENTOR(S) SHOULD be able to help you in four main areas.

Connect you with the right people

SINCE WE'RE IN A COURSE on networking, let's start with this point. Your mentor should be someone who is well-connected **in the ecosystem** you are interested in, and who will be willing to share their connections with you. It will help you network with the right people and expand your network where it is relevant.

Convey the right mindset and inspire you to take action

WHEN IT COMES TO JOB searches or professional opportunities, having a positive mindset sometimes matters just as much as having the right skills. A mentor should help you develop this mindset and **increase your self-confidence** to take action in the right conditions.

Passing on skills to you

A MENTOR IS USUALLY someone who has been successful in the industry or position you are aiming for. As a result, they will be better able to tell you which **skills** and **knowledge** have been most useful for their career. This will allow you to focus on them and learn from their personal experience.

They will also be able to advise you on books, courses, videos, etc., that have had an impact on their career; You can, why not, discuss it together.

Your mentor will help you learn new skills!

Have an external point of view

NOT PART OF YOUR ORGANIZATION or your circle of friends or close acquaintances, your mentor will be able to bring you a **different perspective** on the topics you will present. More objective, because it is not influenced by certain biases, it can really help you progress, challenge yourself and question yourself.

Active mentor and passive mentor?

THERE ARE GENERALLY two types of mentoring: active and passive.

Mentored passif

*The passive mentor is actually someone you **don't know personally**, but who will inspire you with their publications, articles, books, speeches, videos... There are many of them, more or less known, on very generic themes or on more specific subjects.*

TO BENEFIT FROM THEIR best advice, your first job will be to identify them, then identify the platforms and networks on which they communicate (podcasts, videos, books, conferences, etc.) and follow their publications assiduously.

You'll notice that even on this type of mentorship, you'll learn new skills, be inspired to take action, and discover new people.

A great example of this is author Tim Ferriss. After several books, numerous podcasts, videos and conferences, he published at the end of 2016 "Tools of Titans" in which several dozen business leaders, authors, celebrities, athletes, etc., share their advice on how to be more efficient.

Mentees actif

*An active mentor is, as you can see, someone with whom you will have **a direct relationship**. Someone you know, who knows you, who has agreed to play this role and with whom you will exchange regularly.*

NOTE THAT YOU CAN HAVE **several mentors** active at the same time, who will accompany you on different aspects of your projects.

*Be careful, however, **not to want to have too many**, you risk spending less time with everyone and therefore not maintaining quality relationships, which is the objective in* *your networking strategy. In an active mentoring relationship, you also need to **bring value to** the relationship to maintain it; with too many mentors, this is complicated.*

How do I find a good (active) mentor for me?

• First of all, define precisely the part of your project on which you want to be supported as well as the field of action you will propose to your mentor.

• Then do some **research**, at events or via social media, especially to identify interesting profiles. Refer to your personas. A good mentor will usually be **someone who has succeeded** where you want to go. Isolate the identified profiles and validate that they are relevant, with an order of preference, for example.

• **Contact** the identified person(s). Don't be afraid to be clear about your request and go for it, even if you don't know the person. Explain the "why" behind you and why you think this relationship could be interesting.

• Validate the relationship by **talking to the person**. This is an essential moment. If you have a positive response, don't consider yourself a mentor until you've spoken with them. During this exchange, validate the commitment of your interlocutor, the time he or she will be able to devote to you, his or her real skills on the subjects that interest you, the manner and regularity with which you will exchange and above all his or her **values**, in which you must find yourself... Be sure to mark out the relationship well to avoid being disappointed later on.

● Then let the relationship develop by sending regular updates or requests to your mentor. Depending on their answers, you will know very quickly if you have made the right choice and whether or not the relationship with this person in your network will become a true mentor-mentee relationship.

Reverse mentoring ?

FOR SEVERAL YEARS NOW, and the generalization of this notion of mentoring, another concept has emerged, that of "**reverse mentoring**".

> *In this relationship, an **experienced person**, often with an important role in a company, will benefit from the advice of younger people, often students or young professionals.*

It is above all the emergence of digital technology that has contributed to the emergence of this concept. Very often, business leaders, with little training in new technologies, will be accompanied by young professionals who will share with them the right uses on social media, for example.

Whatever your age and experience, you can call on a mentor, and why not become a **mentor** yourself. As with any relationship in your networking strategy, the relationship with a mentor will be based on **exchange** and **sharing**.

In short

● Choosing a mentor (or mentors) means benefiting from an inspiring vision and experience to help you move forward.

- Active or passive, mentoring is an essential benefit in helping you achieve your goals.

Part 2 - Prepare your networking tools and get started
Chapter V

Check your current tools

You will soon be able to start networking effectively. But before that, there are still some "technical" details to be ironed out.

*Whatever actions you take in your strategy, you're going to become **more visible** to the people you're interested in. In order for them to want to follow through, you need to make a "**good impression**", and for that, everything has to be ready and aligned.*

Imagine meeting someone you've targeted, at an event. You've done your job well beforehand, so you know what this person is interested in, and how to address them.

Since you know that you need **to capture their attention** quickly, you add a little. Your 3 years of activity in social media becomes 10 years, and from community manager, you go from director of digital strategy. Once back in his office, and eager to continue the discussion with you, this person finds you on the internet and discovers your "real" profile.

Do you think this relationship is here to stay?

Similarly, imagine that you send a request to a digital marketing director explaining that you want to work in this industry and that you would like to hear their opinion on the latest trends. If your LinkedIn profile explains that you're currently a human resources student, there's little chance that this request will be taken seriously because of the obvious mismatch.

So you have to make sure that doesn't happen. You may not have had time to work on your professional brand in depth.

Don't worry. A few quick but effective actions can help you ensure an **optimal image**, especially on the internet and social networks. Here's how, in a few simple steps.

Clearly define the image you want to convey

DEPENDING ON THE GOALS you have set for yourself and the profiles you want to network with, define the information that should come out of your profile. Make a list of a dozen **keywords, technical skills**, but also **character traits** and human qualities.

> *Be **authentic** in this exercise. Don't decide that a character trait should stand out because it would be good for your profile if it doesn't really fit you. The same goes for a skill you don't master. This is bound to show at some point and could damage the relationships you've built.*

Check how you appear today

DO WHAT THE PEOPLE you're going to network with will do: **search for your name** in search engines. Don't hesitate to add certain keywords (company, school, network, etc.) so you don't miss any results.

In the same way, look at web results as well as **images, videos** and possibly **news**. Don't go very far in the results pages, focus on the first two pages, and especially the first one, since many won't make it.

Repeat this action every 3 to 6 months to see how the results evolve. Algorithms change regularly, and hidden information could come to the surface, jeopardizing all your efforts.

Compare **the search results** with the **keywords** you defined beforehand. If the two are aligned, well done, you just have to maintain that. If not, don't panic, a few quick actions can help you fix it.

Remove anything that is too far away or could harm you

DURING THIS SEARCH, you will probably find **social profiles** that you **no longer use,** or have never used. Unless you've developed a network there that fits your goals, don't hesitate, **delete them**.

In the same way, if you have given reviews that are too negative, if you have posted inappropriate images or comments that could **harm your image**, hide them, or delete them permanently.

If other people have posted things about you (on a blog, a news site, etc.) that go against your strategy, ask them to remove them. In the worst-case scenario, turn to the CNIL, which will be able to take action.

Protect your private spaces

SOME NETWORKS MAY REMAIN outside of your networking strategy. Your avatar on an online gaming platform, your artist profile on SoundCloud, or even just your Facebook profile, for example. If so, make sure to **set** your **privacy preferences** so that everything you share and exchange there doesn't show up in search results.

Protect your private spaces with privacy settings

Optimize the spaces you need to be in

ONCE YOU'VE TAKEN THE right actions to avoid as much as possible the feedback of information that you don't want to appear in the search results, it's time to think now about the information you want to find there! You will, of course, focus on the **spaces** that you have identified as **the most relevant** to you in chapter 1.3.

Connect to the different profiles and media that you will use to network and optimize them to best match the criteria you defined in the first step.

Also, make sure they're **in line with reality** (don't exaggerate!), up-to-date, and aligned. For example, choose a recent profile picture, which highlights you and which you will use on the different spaces.

*If it's relevant, don't hesitate to **create links** between the different spaces to ensure that the people who will join one of* *your networks will also be able to go further, thus strengthening the bond you have just created.*

For example, if we go back to the analysis made in the previous chapters, the priority will be to make sure that my profile in the alumni directory is up to date, has the right contact information and links to my professional profiles, LinkedIn and Twitter in priority (themselves up to date!).

I will therefore send this information to the managers and follow the update of my online profile, and when the next physical directory is published.

Also check and optimize your offline tools

IN YOUR NETWORKING strategy, you will surely include **face-to-face** actions (participation in an event, a conference, etc.). we'll come back to that). For these situations, other tools will be added to the ones you have deployed online.

Again, you will need to make sure that these tools are up-to-date and aligned with your digital presence:

- **Business card:** Professional, with a link to one or two relevant social profiles and up-to-date contact information.

- **Resume:** Can be useful if you want a contact to connect you with a recruiter you've identified, for example. Again, it must be up-to-date and include the same information as on your professional profiles.

- **Your style:** This may sound silly, but if you have long hair and all your profiles are short, it can be confusing.

● **Your way of expressing yourself:** if you speak a common language during the event and your digital presence uses a more sustained lexical field, here again, the discrepancy can be unsettling.

In short

● Present yourself in the best possible light. Online or offline, check and update your image and messages according to your goals.

● LinkedIn is the main professional showcase, the central hub of your networking strategy.

Chapter VI

Take care of your presence on LinkedIn

One of your key tools, which you're going to need to optimize to get the most out of it, will be your LinkedIn presence .

With more than 560 million members in 2018 (updated statistics here) including more than 17 million in France, 2 new members per second and billions of exchanges and information sharing, it is an **essential platform** to make yourself visible and credible, and build your network. Here's how to get the most out of it.

Think of it as a showcase. If it is **attractive** and makes you want to enter your world (your store), you will increase your ability to build a quality network. Your profile should go much further than just a resume. It should **value your experiences** by emphasizing the value you add to your contacts, and how you will be able to help them.

Think back to the goals you set at the beginning of this course. Also, think back to the **keywords** you identified in the previous chapter. All of this should be very clear when reading your profile.

Skills, experience, education, resume, title, etc., must clearly demonstrate what a professional relationship with you will be like. So add your keywords, or synonyms, while of course staying true to your background.

HERE ARE THE KEY POINTS to keep in mind:

- **Profile picture** : professional, that really looks like you (updated), where you are alone.

- **Background visual** : to clearly show your visitors the world they are entering.

- **Title** : By default, your current position, to be customized to talk about the value you offer to your network.

- **Summary** : Explain your passions, your professional background and the expectations you have on the network.

- **Experiences** : Share concrete details of your accomplishments and accomplishments.

- **Skills** : add your key skills, recommend those in your network, get recommended.

- **Recommendations** : Don't hesitate to ask contacts with whom you have already worked to explain in a few words the value of the exchanges you have had.

- **Training** : to show where you come from, to be able to use the alumni network on LinkedIn more easily and to make the most of the diplomas related to your project.

- **Licenses and certifications:** to promote knowledge and learning developed during online training, for example OpenClassrooms courses.

- **Media** : For your summary, your experiences or your studies, add videos, presentations, links, which illustrate what you have written.

- **Other** : passions, languages, volunteer experiences, academic or personal projects... Add anything that may seem relevant to you to enhance your skills and personality and create strong relationships with the people who can help you achieve your goals.

LinkedIn will be a great ally in your networking strategy.

Use Groups

ON LINKEDIN, YOU WILL find **groups** around almost all professional topics. So there's bound to be at least one that fits your networking goals. Search for them in the LinkedIn search engine using keywords and ask to join the ones that seem most relevant.

*Choose groups where there are a **large number of members**, you are more likely to have activity. Since your goal is to expand your network, the more members there are, the more potential connections you will have.*

Once you've been accepted into the group, check the dates of the last posts and the number of engagements. If they go back a long time and/or there are few commitments, this group is not very active and therefore not necessarily a good investment of your time.

Being part of a group is also the opportunity to interact directly with members who have caught your attention without you even needing to be connected with them. A very useful ease of contact... that shouldn't stop you from sharing your respective networks afterwards.

USE GROUPS TO:

- Discover, exchange, and connect with other like-minded LinkedIn members.

- Share your monitoring or publications with a target audience, to gain visibility and credibility.

- Keep you informed of the latest news in specific sectors.

- Seek advice from a community of specialists who can help you.

Build Your News Feed

ALTHOUGH IT'S GOVERNED by a fairly complex algorithm, you can still decide, to some degree, what information you want to see in your LinkedIn news feed.

Here are some "news feed" tips to help you with your networking strategy:

- **Follow the people you want to network with**: You don't have to be connected with someone to see their posts. You can simply "follow" it. Do this for some key people you want to network with. This way, you'll know more about them and be more impactful the day you meet them, or when you add them to your LinkedIn network.

● **Follow influencers** : Many opinion leaders (politicians, business leaders, media directors, etc.) regularly share on LinkedIn. Follow those who might be passive mentors for you and also find out what other professionals they often interact with.

● **Follow #hashtags** : Subscribe to topics that interest you, such as your industry or target position, to find out who is speaking out on those topics. You keep up to date and discover people with whom it might be interesting to network.

● **Follow businesses** : Similar to influencers, many companies regularly share content on LinkedIn. Follow the ones you've identified as interesting, stay informed, and discover people from those companies that you could network with.

The News Feed also gives you an opportunity to communicate. **You, too, are interesting**. You too have things to say, relevant information to share. Communicating is a unique opportunity to arouse the curiosity of LinkedIn members, to get noticed, to establish your credibility and to make new useful contacts. Let's not forget that networking involves giving as much as receiving. Your communications will be taken as gifts that you give to your targets.

Here are the three main ways to communicate on LinkedIn:

Poster:

YOU CAN DISSEMINATE information, share a testimony, offer your services for a job, ask for support, make your state of mind known... A whole range of expression formats are easily accessible to you. In writing, in video, in animation, in photos, in multi-page documents using the carousel. You don't have to be a communications professional to express yourself. A short, well-constructed text, an effective photo to call out, and that's it!

Comment on a post:

GIVE YOUR OPINION ON a post, interact with its author in a public way, ask him a question. You will be able to generate interest and get noticed positively. A simple comment on a post is richer than a like and can create opportunities.

For example, a student who landed her work-study program after being spotted thanks to a simple comment on a post by a company manager. However, he had not made an announcement.

Share:

SINCE THE VERY PURPOSE of the network is to share, take advantage of LinkedIn to offer your current contacts but also to other people content that interests you. Have you read an article on LinkedIn or on a website where you are doing something that you are passionate about? Share it by explaining what captivated you. Your network will no doubt be delighted with this information, you will have developed your visibility and your professional image will have benefited.

Expand your network

OF COURSE, LINKEDIN is also (and especially in the context of this course!) a fantastic tool to **expand your network** and connect with new people who can help you achieve your goals. If you've followed all of the previous steps, you're in a good position to make connection requests that will be accepted, and thus expand your network.

*While some time ago requests were almost systematically accepted, the trend is now towards the **selection of contacts**. More and more users have become aware that accepting someone into your network means sharing a certain amount of information with them. Many are now paying more attention.*

*Don't make bulk add requests. This can lead to your **profile being blocked**, especially if many of the people you've added click on "I don't know this person". So be selective!*

Only ask for people you really know, with whom you share something (relationship, group, interest, company, etc.) or with whom you have a good connection (because you will have researched).

In any case, always **personalize** your invitation. When you click on "Log in", you will be able to add a note to your request. Take advantage of this opportunity, it's your first opportunity to communicate with the person you're interested in. Take the time to **carefully review** their profile. This is a good way to show him that you are interested in this person. **Explain why** you want to get in touch with them and what you can do for each other. Be clear, efficient and concise, you have 300 characters. Don't be commercial in any way.

Here are some examples of network sharing requests:

Example of a personalized invitation for someone with whom you have mutual acquaintances:

"Hi Mr./Mrs. {name}, I see we both know [person's name]. Would you be interested in joining my network to discuss our sectors of activity? In the meantime, I wish you a great day."

Example of a personalized invitation for a recruitment:

"Hello Mr. / Mrs. {name}

While browsing through posts on LinkedIn, I noticed that you are looking for someone for a [job title] position. I have a degree in [name of training or degree] and am looking for a contract in [type of contract]. Can we quickly discuss this recruitment? Thank you in advance and wish you a great day."

Example of a personalized invitation for a person whose profession, career path or company interests you:

"Hello Mr. / Mrs. {name}

I see you've been [job title] for x years. I myself work in this trade / I am currently training to become [title of the profession of the person concerned]. I would love to talk to you about that. Would you be willing to share your experiences with me? Thank you in advance and wish you a great day."

Even if the person adds you without replying or maybe even reading your message, it will remain in your exchanges. So, if you **contact** this person even several months later, they will always have that first message and they will easily remember who you are and why you should follow up.

On mobile, if you click on "connect", it sends the request directly, without leaving you the possibility to customize it. To do this,

*click on the "More..." right next to the login button and choose
the "Customize Invitation" option.*

Be just as **rigorous** and **selective** for incoming requests. Filter to keep
only people with whom you will actually be able to exchange. If it's
not clear, if you don't know the person and don't see what you have
in common, don't hesitate to send them a message to confirm mutual
interest.

Again, this first exchange will remain in your message history and you
will quickly find it again when you get in touch with this person again.

Bonus (premium feature): Look at who has seen your profile.

If you are a premium subscriber, you have the option to see **who has
viewed your profile** over the past few months. Feel free to check out
these people's profiles, and if they're interesting, add them to your
network using this visit as a valid reason to connect!

In short

- As the number one professional social network, LinkedIn
is essential in your network strategy.

- A perfectly developed profile, regular network activity,
effective communication: three major ingredients to achieve
your objectives.

Chapter VII

Use LinkedIn's search function effectively

L inkedIn is the leading professional social network. It's a wealth of information and opportunities that will come in handy every day. To find clients, to apply for an ad or to locate a company for an unsolicited application, to get advice from professionals on a profession, a company, a sector of activity. However, you need to know how to make the best use of LinkedIn's search tool.

Use the different search tabs

A SIMPLE SEARCH BY keywords and LinkedIn offers you people, companies, schools, groups, editorial content, jobs.

Let's look at an example:

> You are a web developer in Lyon and you are looking to expand your network in this field.

Type "web developer Lyon" in the search bar. LinkedIn brings up a multitude of results. Quantity is good, but you may get lost in this ocean of information. Luckily, LinkedIn has you covered. A series of tabs are available to help you sort and refine your search:

- **People:** to select all web developer profiles with the mention Lyon. LinkedIn offers you professionals working in companies or not employees, former professionals, students in training.

- **Posts** : to find all the editorial content about web developer and Lyon.

- **Jobs** : To find job openings in that area and city.

- **Groups** : to find groups around this profession and this city. Joining groups gives you the opportunity to exchange with your peers about common professional interests.

- **Companies** : to discover companies that employ professionals in this field in Lyon.

- **Schools** : to find schools that train in this field.

- **Courses** : for courses on the topic offered by LinkedIn's training entity, LinkedIn Learning.

- **Events** : the opportunity to find business or recruitment events.

- **Services** : the opportunity to identify professionals who offer their services in this field....

A final tab gives you the opportunity to go even further in precision and sorting. The "**All Filters**" tab. You can refine your search according to new criteria:

- **Level of relationship with you:** 1st (people actually in your network); 2nd (people connected with your level 1 contacts); 3rd (people connected with level 2 contacts).

- **Locations:** to find a person by city or region, for example.

- **Contact's current or previous company**

- **School**

- **Sector of activity**

- **Profile Language**

- **Categories of Services**

- **Keywords:** first name, last name, position, company or school of the person sought.

The different tabs under the Linkedin search bar

USING THESE TABS AND filters offers results that are more in line with your expectations. It is also a source of **pleasant surprises**. Are you looking for a job, work-study program or internship? Pay attention to the following.

Take advantage of the "post" tab

THE SEARCH HABIT IS to use the "jobs" tab to find ads related to your project. This reflex is good, but not enough. Many recruiters advertise directly **in posts**. To find them, nothing could be simpler:

1. Type in the keywords of your search. For example, "work-study as a web developer".
2. Sort the results via the "Posts" tab. You will immediately be able to access all posts that contain the words in your search.

*Without this search, you wouldn't find them in the Jobs tab or in the news feed feed. **An additional benefit** : the recruiter's* *email or direct phone contact sometimes appears in the post. All you have to do is go ahead and apply!*

Leverage Boolean operators

ANOTHER WAY TO QUICKLY achieve qualified results is **Boolean operators.** Behind this word, which is mysterious to some, hides a very simple and already old system to refine your searches on a classic search engine, and that LinkedIn has taken over. A Boolean operator allows you to combine several elements or limit your search to certain aspects. In short, to **find a treasure** without stirring up all the sand of the desert island on which it is buried!

There are several operators. Let's take a look at some of them below.

Quotation marks

IF YOU SEARCH FOR PROFILES with *a digital marketing manager* title without using quotation marks, you may end up with what you're looking for, but more.

> *For example, for profiles with the word responsible, such as communication managers. Essential information will be drowned out in the mass. The use of quotation marks around your search, "digital communication manager" ensures you qualified answers.*

OR and AND inclusions and NOT exclusion

THESE BOOLEAN OPERATORS allow you to associate elements. They should always be used in capital letters.

AND operator: Enter the word to get the results that contain all the items in the search.

Example: With **"communication manager" AND digital,
you get profiles that contain both "marketing manager"
and the word "digital".**

OR operator: Enter the word to see results that include at least one
element of your query.

Example: **"communication manager" OR
"communications director",** the results show profiles that
contain one **or** the other of these expressions.

NOT operator: type it into the engine before the term you are looking
for, this excludes it from your results.

Example: **"marketing communication manager" NOT
assistant**. You will only get the marketing communication
managers, without being polluted by the marketing
communication manager assistants.

Consider limited searches

BE CAREFUL, THE FREE version of LinkedIn sets **search limits** :
it is impossible for you to do as many as you want in a set amount of
time. An additional difficulty is that this limit is not known. LinkedIn's
algorithm is a mystery, and to complicate matters, it changes regularly.
All you have to do is adapt.

If LinkedIn notifies you that you're reaching the limit, you have two
options:

- Wait a few days to be allowed to search again;

- Take a Premium membership to get around this limit.

The choice is yours, but you should know that it is possible to be active on LinkedIn without taking out a subscription.

If you use LinkedIn's search function, think that others are doing it as well. That is, it's in your best interest to be found by other users. The solution: have the keyword reflex. Only a profile rich in information, perfectly informed and taking into account the keywords of your profession or your sector of activity will allow you to stand out in the results of the LinkedIn search engine.

Boost your search results.

ON LINKEDIN, THE IMAGE you convey is crucial to helping you achieve your goals. As we have seen, the quality of your profile is essential. It must be rich, complete, and have the keywords of your profession to allow you to be spotted and to capture attention.

Your image, but also the effectiveness of your actions on LinkedIn, also depend on the richness of your network. If your network is quantitatively very limited, the results of your searches by the LinkedIn engine will be just as limited. So be careful **to develop your network enough to make the most of the search tool**.

Set an initial contact goal, such as two hundred.

In short

- Finding a needle in a hayland is much easier with the LinkedIn search tool.

- Use the sorting tabs and Boolean operators to come to your rescue.

Chapitre VIII

Implement your online strategy

You have now started networking using LinkedIn. While you're likely to spend a lot of your time on it, don't forget that there are **other tools** and networks that can fit into your strategy.

Indeed, even if they may seem less "professional" at first, many social networks can be very useful to you. More and more **mobile apps** can also help you find the right people **nearby**. Let's take a look.

The use of social networks

JUST LIKE LINKEDIN, using other networks should allow you to get closer to the people who can help you achieve your goals. So keep these in mind as you think about which networks are relevant to you.

Depending on your goals, some networks will be more relevant than others.

For example, if you are looking to network in the music industry, a network like SoundCloud will certainly be more interesting than a network dedicated to images. If you want to connect with video influencers, you'll favor YouTube or possibly Instagram. It's up to you to choose what seems **most relevant** to your goals.

Generally speaking, you will use social networks to connect with the people you are interested in, exchange with them, but also, and above all, in most cases, to keep up to date with the **news** of these people or the sector you are targeting.

Twitter

ON TWITTER, FIRST FOLLOW the various media outlets that share news about the sector of activity or function you are interested in. In addition to keeping you informed, this will allow you to discover **interesting people** who react to tweets from these media outlets, and follow them as well.

> *Don't hesitate to search by **keywords** and **hashtags** to find interesting people, who share on the topics that interest you, and discover influencers that you can then contact directly. Create **lists** to easily and quickly find the people, roles or topics that interest you.*

Of course, look for and follow the people you have met or discovered through other channels (physically or on other networks), because it is a channel, which often mixes professional and personal, that will allow you to get to know people better in order to better network with them. Finally, **share information**, tag (with @) people with whom you want to exchange.

Twitter is a fast-paced platform that works very well at events, for example. The **media**, **companies** and **opinion leaders** also share a lot, often with a certain proximity.

Use this power to discover new people to connect with and better understand the people, companies, roles, or industries you're interested in to enrich your direct exchanges.

Facebook

> *Don't make it a habit to add everyone you've met at events or other social media to Facebook.*

FACEBOOK HAS A VERY personal connotation, and unless you have that person's consent, or the context lends itself to it (informal event, for example), it will often be considered too intrusive.

On the other hand, Facebook can be very powerful in **strengthening existing links** with people you may know too little, former students from your school, for example, with whom you are connected but have never exchanged. The proximity and tone offered by Facebook will then come in handy.

Also, don't hesitate to explore **groups** or pages (of events, companies, etc.) to discover people with whom it might be interesting for you to network.

Respond to their comments, reach out to them directly, if relevant, or learn about more personal aspects before reaching out to them more formally on LinkedIn, for example.

Instagram

ON INSTAGRAM, LOOK for **companies** or influencers (potential passive mentors) first and foremost. The network can be interesting to learn more about the very personal aspects of really key targets, but note that many accounts are private. You may spend a lot of time on it and end up with very little return in terms of network.

If you still want to network there, be aware that you won't necessarily find all the professions and all the sectors of activity that might interest you. Artists, photographers, designers, sports coaches are much more present and visible than professions such as accountants, HR managers or marketers.

So know how to invest time in it in an intelligent way, and in very specific cases where you know that you will be able to find value, and bring it.

Other networks

OTHER NETWORKS, SUCH as **YouTube**, **SoundCloud** or **Snapchat** can also be used in your networking strategy, but often in a less active way. Here again, you will find people or companies that might be interesting and can engage with their content or contact them directly.

> *Many of these "other" networks have either a model or a **very specific target**, whether in terms of sectors of activity, professions, or even "personas".*

For example, if you're looking to network with older business leaders, there's little chance that Snapchat will be the perfect place to reach out to them. Don't forget to take this into account before investing time in identifying contacts and connecting with them on different social networks.

Networking applications

IN RECENT YEARS, WITH the growing number of smartphones and the development of geolocation technologies, for example, new **applications** dedicated to networking have appeared.

Use networking apps

VERY OFTEN INSPIRED by dating apps, they could well help you find new people even faster and network with them effectively, wherever you are.

LinkedIn

WE HAVE ALREADY MENTIONED the network and all the opportunities for exchange it offers. In the mobile app, the "nearby" feature can help you discover other people who are at the same event and have also activated the app. You'll also be able to easily add a contact (or get added) by scanning or sharing the QR code automatically generated by the app.

Shapr ou Ripple

THESE TWO APPS, WHICH work on the principle of "**match**", like Tinder (Ripple was created by Tinder's executives and financed by its parent company), will allow you to get in touch with **hyper-targeted profiles.**

Only a few profiles are offered to you every day, and you have to say whether or not you would be interested in a meeting or exchange. If it is reciprocal, then you can follow the discussion.

In both cases, you **set up** a certain amount of information, keywords, sectors of activity, professions, etc., to help the algorithm offer you relevant profiles. It's often quite impressive in terms of the quality of the profiles offered!

These apps can allow you to go beyond the networks you'd naturally think of and discover people you would never have contacted otherwise.

Meetup

THE PRINCIPLE OF THE app is simple: allow you to network with people who share the same interests as you. Log in as a user or create your own Meetups if you want to go further!

The app will allow you to join **discussion groups** on professional topics, find running partners, or why not, join **events** organized in your area, or wherever you will be on the go.

Again, set up the app by indicating the topics you are interested in and joining groups.

As soon as a relevant event is offered, you will receive a notification and can register. Great for meeting new people.

Bizzabo or Eventbrite

IF YOU PREFER TO NETWORK "in real life", you may also find interest in these applications, used by many **event organizers**.

Not only will you find all the information about the events, but also the opportunity to meet other people and exchange with them.

Of course, organizing your own networking event can also be a possibility; In that case, these apps could also be ideal!

There are many other apps to help you with your networking: a smart address book to get all the details about the people you meet, an interactive map to find out which events your network is going to or a matching app to find a lunch buddy, for example.

It's up to you to try the available applications that seem interesting to you to see if they are really useful and help you network!

In short

- Boost your networking strategy with social media and mobile apps. They are an inexhaustible source of information, exchange and openness.

- Choose the platforms that best meet your goals.

Chapter IX

Adopt the right behavior

All your networking tools are now ready. You've decided on a strategy and started connecting with other people, especially through social media. In order to be sure that all these efforts pay off, it is important not to make any "missteps".

On social media, everything moves very quickly, and the slightest mistake, even if made unintentionally, can very quickly be amplified and all your efforts can be undermined.

In order to avoid these inconveniences, here are some **very simple and practical reflexes** that you should keep in mind when networking on social media.

Customize

WHEN MAKING CONNECTION requests or getting in touch with someone on social media, **always personalize** your request or message.

Don't just copy and paste where you would change the person's name.

Personalize your approach, why you're looking to connect with that person specifically, what interests you about them...

Tell yourself that non-personalized requests are still the norm and very common on social networks. Also, customizing yours will directly give you an **advantage** and allow you to be immediately remarkable, and different!

Do your research

BEFORE YOU CONNECT with someone, and to be able to best customize your request, make sure you have enough **information** to be relevant. Look at the person's profiles, their posts, their website if they have one, the recommendations they may have received...

Use all of this to write messages that will actually hit the mark. Be inspired by the lexical field used by this person so that they can be found in the request or message you will send, for example.

All this may take a little time, but it is **necessary** to gain the trust of the people with whom you want to network and build quality exchanges.

Be patient, don't automate your networking

IT CAN BE TEMPTING to speed up your networking by inviting your address book en masse or by sending massive requests for connections on certain networks, via plugins in particular.

> *You should avoid these practices as much as possible. Aim for* ***quality*** *over quantity.*

In addition to the fact that these practices are illegal on most networks, and could lead to the **suspension** or **deletion of your accounts**, they are above all contrary to a personalized and strategic approach that meets specific objectives. This could lead to the risk of being connected to the wrong people and/or having an unusable network, which you would not be able to contact with them.

> *What could be more infuriating than seeing that someone in your network can put you in touch with the CEO of the*

*company you're targeting, but that relationship isn't strong
enough to be able to make that request?*

Open

AS YOU UNDERSTOOD FROM the introduction, networking is
all about human relationships. As such, don't be afraid to be yourself,
to be authentic, even if it means you're going to have to indulge a little.

If you try to be too "smooth", too professional or corporate, you don't
make visible what **differentiates** you and makes you **unique**.

On social media, as well as at events, share your story and emphasize
the points that will make you **memorable**. It can be a particular
experience, an expertise, a character trait, a way of expressing yourself
or, why not, a color of clothing.

> *No one wants to network with a robot, let alone open up to it.
> To network successfully, you need others to open up to you to
> understand them better. Don't hesitate to take the first step!*

Give, give, give... then ask

TO BUILD QUALITY RELATIONSHIPS that will last over time,
don't over-solicit your network. Before you ask Him for anything, you
must first give, give, and give some more.

Whether it's content, advice, networking, feedback, be **generous** with
your network, they will reciprocate. You have to somehow "earn" the
right to ask.

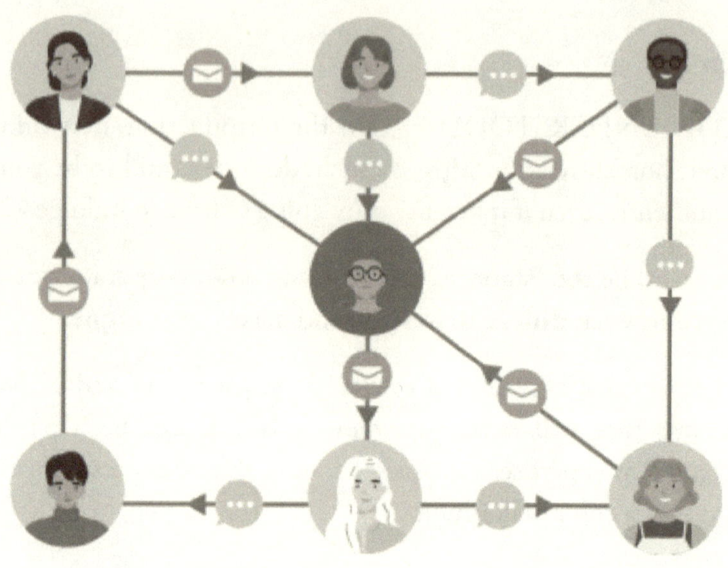

Reciprocity will come, start by giving!

ON SOCIAL MEDIA, THE principle of "**reciprocity**" is often used as law. We follow the people who follow us (follow back), we recommend people who have recommended us... Also enter into this logic, do not hesitate to help your network in a selfless way to gain its trust and then benefit from the effects of this principle.

Pay attention to the number of contacts

THIS DATA IS USUALLY visible on most networks. So, in just a few seconds, when they land on your profiles, the people you're looking to network with will get an idea of the type of network you're looking to build.

Too many contacts? You are a "collector" and cannot bring value to all. Few contacts? You're a beginner who can't provide enough value yet.

In the same way, if you follow thousands of people, but no one follows you back, it sends a negative signal. Either you've selected the wrong people or you're not interesting.

So always try to have a **balanced ratio**, and to maintain a network that allows for rich personal exchanges.

Join the conversation

DON'T JUST BE JUST another contact. Be one of those your network sees regularly, for the right reasons.

Don't just push information, **take part in the exchanges** that take place on the network you have chosen.

Like, reply, interact, ask questions, restart the discussion... Don't hesitate to be active in the groups you have joined and in your contacts' mailboxes.

Be responsive, follow the exchanges

SOCIAL MEDIA IS A PLACE of "real time". You can't afford to wait months or even weeks or days for a request or message.

So be present on a regular basis and follow the exchanges you have as much as possible. The quality of your network also depends on your **responsiveness.**

Imagine you're going to an event. A person adds you to a network, following this first meeting, with a lot of things in mind to ask you. If you confirm this request several months later, it's a safe bet that she will have found answers to her questions. You will have missed a great opportunity to create a strong relationship!

> *Don't be "too" reactive either! There's nothing worse, after confirming a new relationship, than receiving a pre-formatted, non-personalized commercial message a few seconds later ! Don't be one of those people who get off to a bad start because you're rushing in without listening to your contacts.*

Don't be too restrictive, be curious!

NETWORKING IS ALSO a matter of **curiosity** and **open-mindedness**. Of course, you have your personas and goals, but don't hesitate from time to time to let yourself be surprised by less "conventional" or less expected relationships.

You don't know where these relationships will take you and what the networks of these people are. So don't systematically refuse relationships that don't fit into your scheme. At worst, you can always remove that relationship or hide its posts if it turns out to be uninteresting or "polluting" to your news feed.

In short

- Adopting best practices is the assurance of building quality relationships, in the service of your objectives.

- Be human, open, attentive, interesting, patient and outward-looking. Donate, on social media as well as in person, and you will receive.

Part 3 - Nurture Your Professional Network

Chapter X

―――

Expand your current network

Now you know where your networking strategy should take you. You've sharpened your tools to make this possible and you've even started networking on some networks. Well done!

Now it's time to get into the final phase and really **grow** your network. To get started, you'll start by selecting the right strategy, and starting from what you've already built and analyzed: your **current network**.

Let's take a look at how to capitalize on what already exists to develop it, help you reach your goals faster and connect with the right people, in a smart and strategic way.

Choose the "direction" of your networking

NETWORKING IN, UP, out, down? Inbound or outbound networking? You may have already wondered which strategy **is best** suited to your goals... Or not!

Indeed, what do these terms really mean, and in which case should this or that strategy be used? And why not use multiple strategies at the same time to network effectively?

Networking in ou out ?

TWO SOLUTIONS WILL be open to you. Network in what you already know, "in", or go further into the unknown: "out".

If you're looking to **move forward** in your company, for example, you're going to adopt an "in" strategy by connecting with people in the company, or improving the relationships you already have there. The same goes for when you're looking to evolve in your industry: you'll be looking to interact with people who are also there.

If, on the other hand, you are looking **to change your career path**, or if you want to open up new perspectives, you will have to look for connections in other networks or fields of activity.

> *An "out" approach will seem more complicated to set up, because it requires you to get out of your comfort zone and exchange with new people, who do not necessarily have the same codes.*

> *Of course, it is possible to **combine** an "in" and an "out" approach to achieve long-term goals. For example, if you want to become a manager in your company, you will network internally, to gain visibility with the right people, but also externally to find other inspiring managers who can share their best practices and help you progress.*

Networking up ou down ?

IN MOST CASES, YOU will seek to get in touch with people who have a higher hierarchical responsibility than you (networking up), as these are often the people who can help you **achieve your goals** and **inspire you**.

However, in some cases, creating relationships with people who are less advanced in their careers, or at the same level, can also be relevant.

For example, if you want to **become a manager** of a team, maintaining good relationships with the people of this team or having an equivalent level will allow you to better position yourself in the process, or to better understand their challenges in order to better respond to them.

If you are in a reverse mentoring approach, networking with students or young people at the beginning of their careers can also pay off.

When you're in an "**up**" gait, it's normal to be a little **uncomfortable**. Some specialists will tell you that if you're not, you're not aiming high enough, so challenge yourself!

In a "**down**" approach, the risk is sometimes to show **complacency** or superiority. Be careful with this, the effect on the relationships you create is bound to be negative.

Inbound ou outbound networking ?

IF YOU'RE NOT VERY comfortable with the idea of networking and the risk-taking that comes with it, maybe you'll decide to take an "**inbound**" approach.

As in marketing and communication, this means that you will try to **attract** people to your network rather than going to them ("outbound" approach).

By providing value and sharing information with your current network, you will be visible and credible to other relationships who will be looking to join your network.

*An **inbound** strategy is interesting because it is particularly rewarding for you. On the other hand, it will require more **time** and **energy** than a strategy where you would be the one to meet the people you are interested in.*

Also, how do you make sure that the most relevant people will actually be the ones who come to you? So don't hesitate to **mix the two strategies**, by enhancing your image, but also by getting in touch directly with the people you have identified.

Leverage Your "Weak Ties"

*It was in 1973 that the American sociologist Mark Granovetter was the first to mention the existence **of strong** and **weak ties**. According to him, the strength of the bond you have with a person depends on several factors: time spent together, emotional intensity, intimacy and reciprocity. Your strong bonds are therefore your loved ones, family and friends. Your weak ties, mere acquaintances with whom you have a less intense relationship.*

IN THE SAME ARTICLE, Mark Granovetter explains that it is the **weak links**, because of their diversity and the connections they can open, that are the most interesting and relevant to exploit.

With **social media**, the number of these weak links has increased enormously, and you can rely on them permanently and almost instantaneously.

And you, do you know how to recognize these weak ties and solicit them in the best possible way?

To detect these interesting weak links, you will have to go back to the analysis you have made of your networks.

● Look at the contacts with whom you have had little interaction, but who are a good fit for your goals.

● Choose the people who are **the most active and well-connected, as they are the ones who can bring you the most value.**

● Seek to understand who they are connected to, how strong these relationships are. For example, look at their recent posts, the engagement they have received (likes, shares, comments, etc.) and who the people who generated these engagements.

Your goal is to understand how you will be able to rely on these weak links to **gain visibility** with the right people, either because they will reshare your content with their network, or by asking them to put them **in direct contact**, because you know that they have a great proximity to your **strategic targets.**

*As such, don't hesitate to ask these contacts to help you connect with people in **their networks**. It's a common practice and it works. You'll get better feedback from someone who knows the person than from contacting them directly.*

If you have a possible connection, explore it systematically before making a direct request.

To get as much feedback as possible, here are some best practices to follow in your application:

● Be clear about **why** you want to get in touch with the person in question. Be as specific as possible in your request.

● Show that you've done your research and that you know there's a **mutual interest** in building that relationship.

● Ask for the connection when you know it will have an **impact**. Detect beforehand that the relationship between the two people is strong enough for the proposal to provide an answer. This is especially true when you have several possible connections.

● Offer to write the **introductory message.** Show the person you're asking that you're aware of their time and offer a message that they just need to personalize. In this way, you remove a very important obstacle.

● Always leave a **way out** for the person you are asking. She shouldn't feel like she has no choice, she should be able to say no. This is sometimes preferable to a bad connection.

● **Keep it** up to date with the follow-up to the matchmaking. Whether it's positive or negative, send a message to the person who made the connection to thank them and give them an update. If you apply again in the future, she'll know it's not just one way!

Here's an example:

Title: I finally tried that Italian restaurant you told me about!

Bonjour Angela,

I hope you're doing well. I finally took the time to test this restaurant you told me about, indeed excellent, we enjoyed it! I'm all ears if you have any other advice for my next trip to Paris! Thanks again!

Back to business! I'm looking to get in touch with Nicolas X and I see that you're in touch on LinkedIn. Do you think it is possible to put us in touch? I understood that he was looking for a database management solution, my area of expertise!

To make it easier for you, here's an idea for a message that would work:

> "Hello Nicolas,
>
> I hope your projects are progressing well. Guillaume X, with whom I have worked in the past, would like to get in touch with you.
>
> It seems to me that his company's CRM solutions are well suited to your needs and your company's projects.
>
> I invite you to talk to him, he has availability next Tuesday.
>
> See you soon, Angela."

If that wasn't possible, don't worry, I'll look for another solution. Thank you in advance for your feedback and see you soon!

Guillaume

In short

- We all have a network, and we all have the capacity to develop it. Know how to spot the right people from your existing network, know how to water the seeds, you will see how rich and surprising the harvest can be.

● Social media works for you. Know how to identify the contacts they recommend, you will find new relationships that can help you achieve your goals.

Chapter XI

Bring value to your networks

As you can see, if you are well exploited, your network can bring you a lot. But true to the principles of **reciprocity** and **generosity** seen above, you must also bring value to it to make it effective and make it last over time.

But what exactly do you have to **give** him? What can you offer them to help them evolve and perceive you as an important contact?

Answering these questions may seem even more complicated the younger and inexperienced you will be. Yet, regardless of your age or professional level, the size of your network, or the relationships you've already created, you need to play this game. And don't worry, it's not as complicated as it may seem at first!

Simply go over the elements seen in the first chapter of this course on the reasons that will push you to build your professional network. Simply. Your network is looking to address the **same issues** as you, and this is where you can help:

- to stay informed;

- learn new skills;

- create new opportunities;

- gain visibility and credibility.

And of course, also **respond to** the requests made to you.

If you never respond to direct messages sent to you or requests for connections made to you (even awkwardly, not everyone will have taken this course!), don't expect to be able to call on your network, even if you're trying to bring maximum value to it.

Help your network stay informed

YOU NEED TO BE THE contact your network has in mind when they talk about specific topics. Become the one your network turns to when they have questions or want to stay informed about the latest news in a particular sector, the one you are targeting or on which you want to **position yourself** of course.

Start with an **audit** of your network. What are the themes that seem to interest him most?

To do this, look at the **topics** you see most often. The posts that generate the most engagements, the events that seem to interest your contacts are all keys to understanding these strong interests of your network.

Then look at two dimensions for each of these topics:

- those on which you are legitimate to speak and become a credible channel of information;

- those on which you want to position yourself to achieve your goals.

When these two dimensions intersect, you have topics on which you will be able to share, inform and exchange information with your network.

Then create a **regular watch** on these topics, by isolating key sites or creating alerts on Google or Scoop.it, for example.

Also, feel free to create **your own** thought pieces. Then share on a regular basis all this content that will be relevant to your network and establish your credibility.

The more credible and visible you are on these key topics, the more you can be contacted by your network, but the more you can also attract new people to your network.

Indeed, if the articles shared or written by you are interesting, they will be reshared and amplified with the 2nd and 3rd levels of your contacts' relationship, which will enrich your network.

Be a true "connector" for your network

YOUR CONTACTS HAVE **needs**, and something to **offer**. Whether it's a skill, a business partner, relationships, strategic information... They are just like any professional.

If you can be the person who allows a supply and a demand to meet, you become a valuable asset to your network. And for that, you don't need to have years of experience, you just need to **know how to listen** to your network to become an indispensable contact.

A bit like you have done several times since the beginning of this course, you will look at your different contacts, try to understand what are the **populations** that make it up.

Salespeople? Recruiters? Are you looking for a job? Freelancers? Developers? The more you know who you have in your network, the more you'll be able to foster truly relevant connections.

Also, be sure to validate what you think you know about your relationships, so you don't put the wrong people in contact with each other.

By taking on a "connector" role, you become a weak link that is extremely important to the members of your network.

For example, if you know that you have freelance art directors in your network on the one hand and communication agencies on the other, make sure that you know a minimum of each other's work before putting them in touch.

Then listen to your network. Be present on a regular basis to **detect needs** that are shared on a regular basis.

- Are you looking for a CRM? Tag your sales contact at a software company.

- Another wonders how to become a self-employed entrepreneur? Share the OpenClassrooms course on the topic with them, or connect them with a contact who has been with them for years.

- A third is looking to establish itself in a particular country? Recommend that they connect with a contact from that country by commenting on their post.

- Finally, is one of them looking for a job? Share their post by tagging some of your recruiter contacts.

By taking on this role of **connector** between all your contacts, you become a particularly strong and important weak link, as you serve as a bridge between different groups that otherwise wouldn't talk to each other. You help create or accelerate **opportunities** for your network and become indispensable and recognized beyond your first level.

Finally, the more you give, the more your network will be willing to help you when you're the one asking.

Enhance your network

HERE IS ANOTHER VERY easy action to do, which will only take you a few minutes, but which will have a very big impact on your network and the relationships you will create.

Networking is first and foremost about developing human relationships. And like any human being, your contacts like to **be seen** and to feel **recognized**. When they share content, like you, they want it to show and generate engagement.

Like and comment on relevant shares in your network. On a daily basis, connect to the networks you have decided to be present on, follow the **thread of discussions** and enter the **conversation**. Like a share, congratulate a promotion, share a post... You become more visible and give visibility to your contact to the rest of your network.

Everyone wants to have someone in their network who knows how to recognize their talents, appreciate them and share them!

> **Another advantage**: *the more you like or comment on posts related to your favorite topics, the more LinkedIn enriches your discussion thread with posts that interest you.*

Also, feel free to **recommend the skills** of the contacts you know best or write a recommendation. On LinkedIn, you can do this directly on the person's profile, or by giving a "well done", which will appear as a public post. On other networks, don't hesitate to make a post tagging the contact you want to thank or congratulate.

In the "Skills & Recommendations" section of your contact, simply click on the "+" next to the skill indicated.

The '+' button of a project management skill turning green, once validated

To write a recommendation from someone you know, it's just as easy.

Would you like to recommend Sophie Durand, your former manager? Click on the "More" tab below their first and last name, then click on "Recommend".

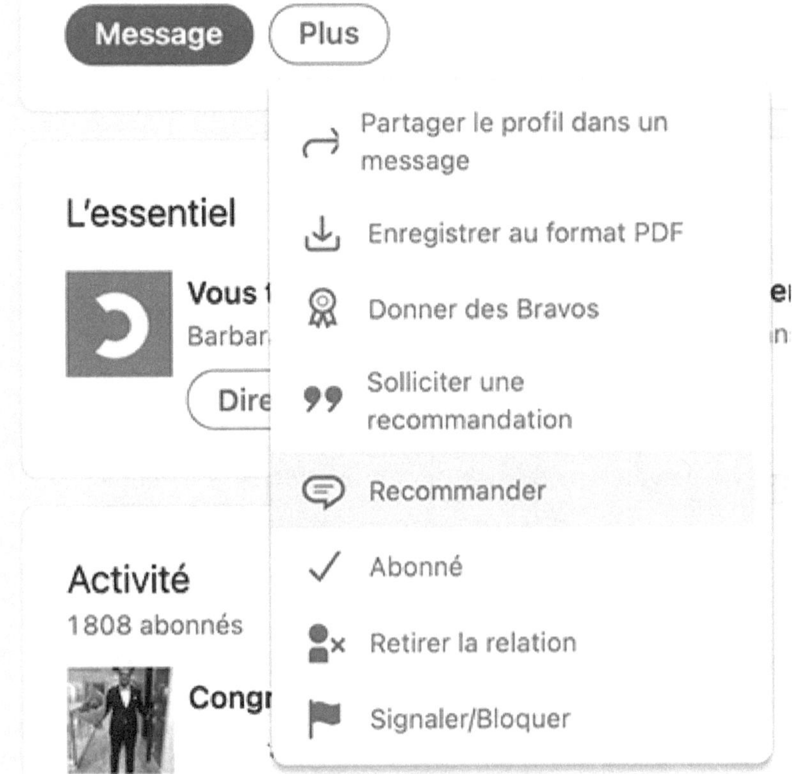

The "recommend" button

Indicate the level of relationship between you.

For example, "You were under Sophie's responsibility". Next, select the position Sophie was holding at the time: manager at *PimPamPom*. Write your recommendation by **highlighting Sophie's technical skills** or human **and** professional **qualities**. They will be delighted to receive your recommendation and have it appear on their LinkedIn profile, in the "Recommendations" section.

One clarification: making a recommendation is only possible if you are connected to this person. You can also give a "well done", which will appear as a public post. It's available through the "More" tab under your contact's name. On other networks, don't hesitate to make a post tagging the contact you want to thank or congratulate.

Bringing value to your network is therefore not as complicated as it may have seemed at first.

And since the principle of the network is to give but also to receive, remember to ask your contacts to **value you**. A recommendation from a manager, a former director or a mentor has never hurt, quite the contrary! The process is exactly the same as recommending, with one difference: on the person's profile, choose "Request a recommendation". All you have to do is write your application. Here's an example:

"Hello Mr./Mrs. *[name]*

I hope you're doing well. Currently looking for a job, I am looking to develop my LinkedIn network and enhance my profile to create opportunities. I would like to know if you would be willing to write me a few lines of recommendation about my *[work, service or service, particular aspect that you may have encountered during the production, reminder of what the client appreciated about you and told you orally...]* Your recommendation will be invaluable in helping me in my research.

Thank you in advance and remain at your disposal for more information."

In short

● Give to your network, share information, recognize successes and talents. This will help you build an image as a credible interlocutor. A real key to ask for your return.

● Be generous and relevant, assert your personality but keep your strategy in mind and avoid an overrated and exaggerated presence. It would scare away your targets and you would miss your goals.

Chapter XII

———

Reach out to your contacts in a smart way

You have now built your network strategically and meaningfully to achieve your goals. You know where you want to go and who can help you get there. You have created a relationship of trust with some key contacts in your network, who are growing in number.

There comes a time when you will probably be the least comfortable, that of **asking your contacts** for something.

Whether you're looking for a job, a contact, information, a recommendation, you're going to have to **contact** people you know little or not at all directly, and it's normal to feel uncomfortable about it. Here are 6 best practices to help you in this process, and make it more effective!

We have already mentioned the request for matchmaking, which obeys very specific codes and has a specific objective, we will see here other types of requests.

Choose the right direct channel

THIS MAY SEEM OBVIOUS, but it's the most important element.

> *The person you contact should not feel that your request is going to require extra effort or that they are not up to your request just because they discover it 1 month late.*

You know the key members of your network, you know where they are and where they interact. Contact them here.

If the contact is very active on LinkedIn, send them an InMail. If he travels frequently to events, meet him there. If you know he likes to talk over the phone and you have his number, give him a call. If you know it's someone who is attached to certain codes, why not send them something in the mail.

> *By using the **right channel**, you increase the possibility of a response and show that you are attentive to the other person.*

Ask for advice

> *When using your network, don't be too direct.*

IF YOU'RE LOOKING FOR a job, contacting a recruiter to ask if they're hiring is a bad idea. At best, they will ask you to send them your CV; at worst, it will ignore your request.

If you want the head of an investment fund to take an interest in your start-up, avoid sending them the link to your website and telling them that you are looking for funds.

> *By being too direct in your request, you are in a **weak position** in relation to your contact.*

You're not in a win-win relationship that will interest them, but in a one-way relationship. You need to pique the person's interest and build a relationship that will help you achieve your goals, but in the longer term. Don't try to close the deal on the first message, but to **start a conversation.**

To take the previous examples, a recruiter will be better able to respond to a request for help in building a professional project, as a recruitment specialist. Similarly, an investor will feel more valued if you ask them what they think of your business plan, having seen dozens of them.

As another example, if you are looking to enter a new position or a new sector of activity, do not hesitate to contact your target companies to ask them to share with you their vision of the sector or the evolution of their functions. You create much stronger and **more interesting** relationships.

Personalize your message

AS YOU CAN SEE, WE can't say it enough: **personalization** is the key to successful networking; this of course also applies to your direct requests.

If your message is too generic or appears like an advertisement, you have almost no chance of getting feedback. Worse, it can jeopardize the entire relationship, as you start with a **serious mistake**.

It is very important to personalize your message

USE ALL THE INFORMATION you've discovered about your target contacts by tracking their news and activities on different networks to personalize your message. Don't hesitate to link your issues to theirs in order to show the relevance of an exchange and the way in which your interests meet.

Don't insist

ON AVERAGE, IF YOU don't get an answer after two direct approaches, consider that the person won't respond to you. Either your request was poorly worded, it wasn't interesting, or the person doesn't have time for you.

> *Insisting can only have a negative effect on the person, who will consider you more like spam and may even take you out of their network.*

If you don't get an answer after a follow-up, **take a step back**. Go back to the basics of networking: **listening** and providing **value**. Wait for the right opportunity(s) to gain visibility with this person, then make your direct request again with this credit.

It takes longer, but it's better not to get an answer right away and to be able to ask again in the future than to point the finger at the person and cut off all contact!

Be Remarkable and Noticed

WHEN YOU MAKE YOUR request, if your contact immediately understands who you are, where you met, how you got into a relationship for example, then you are more likely that they will respond to you easily.

*It is therefore important to have done the work well upstream with a **consistent presence** on all your networks, and to have ensured your **visibility** in your network.*

An example I like to mention is that of a colorful character that I had the opportunity to meet at a few events and that I often saw in the shares of my network, without ever having exchanged with him. His peculiarity is that he always wore a fuchsia sweater. At events, on his profile pictures... Always the same sweater and the same color. The day he contacted me to ask me to participate in a survey he was conducting on social media, I immediately knew who he was and what he was doing, and I responded very quickly. He had removed a number of obstacles and was able to capture my attention well in advance.

Without going that far, find ways to **stand out** when you can, with a tone, a color, an accessory, a style that is unique to you. This will allow the person you're contacting to immediately understand who is making the request and why they need to respond. If it's not obvious, feel free to add it in a very short **introduction** to your post.

Respect your contacts' time

WHEN YOU ASK YOUR NETWORK for something, make sure it's not out of proportion to the **level of relationship** you have or how you've helped them in the past.

You can ask your close friends to spend 20 minutes answering a questionnaire to help you with your career project; You can't make the same request to your weak links.

Make sure your requests are not **time-consuming** for your contacts and make sure that this is very clear to them. "It will only take you a minute", "Can we schedule a telephone conversation of no more than

10 minutes?", "I only have 3 questions to ask you", are all ways to submit your request to show that you have thought about this aspect.

In short

• Choose the right channel, don't be too direct, personalize your messages, stand out from the crowd, be patient... These are all good practices that should open doors for you.

• Dare to make contact and don't project the answers that could be given to you. There is no risk in trying your luck, quite the contrary. The network can be very generous.

Chapitre XIII

Also build your offline network

Social **networks**, mobile apps and the web in general are great tools in your networking strategy. They allow access to contacts without space or time limits and are therefore real **accelerators** to allow you to identify the right people and exchange with them.

But as you've read many times during this course, networking is all about **human interactions** and **relationships**. An online-only strategy is therefore not enough to create long-lasting relationships of trust.

> *You're going to have to leave the comfort of your computer screen and jump into the arena by meeting "for real" the people in your network.*

This is of course a **risk**, but also a great **opportunity**!

Identify the right events

IN ORDER FOR THE TIME spent in person to be effective, you must carefully **select the events** you will attend. Indeed, it requires a greater investment of time and energy than the development of your online network, so you might as well make the most of it.

To choose the most relevant events, you're going to need to do some **research**. Choose events where you are guaranteed to meet people you want to network with.

If you're looking to connect with specific businesses, for example, make sure they'll be present at the event. If you want to create a network in a particular sector of activity, don't miss THE trade show on this theme.

Identify the right events

Depending on your objectives, you can choose rather **large** events, or events in smaller **groups**, such as meet-ups. While the former (trade shows, conferences, etc.) allow you to have more contacts, the latter have the advantage of allowing you to go further in the first exchanges and therefore to know very quickly if the relationship is relevant, while learning more about the person. On a larger event, you'll have less time to deepen the relationship.

To select the best events, of course use the internet, social networks and apps, but don't hesitate to use your network to make sure you select the best events ! This is a simple request that will allow you to exchange with your network.

For example, ask: "Do I have a digital marketing event to recommend to me in Paris?" or "I'm going to the franchise fair for my thesis, someone from my network to have a coffee?" You'll be surprised by the feedback, and you'll be able to play online and offline at the same time.

Prepare to be comfortable

GOING TO AN EVENT, and a professional one at that, can make you **nervous**. Especially since you're going there with the goal of meeting new people.

How to approach them? Will I succeed in being interesting? Who will I be able to talk to? These are all questions that you are probably asking yourself, and that can make you anxious.

Don't panic. Again, it's all about preparation and a few easy little tricks can help you be less stressed.

- **Go with you** : together, we are stronger! Ask a friend, contacts in your network, or professional acquaintances to come with you. Not only will you be more comfortable, but you will also be able to meet their network.

- **Work in advance** : look at who will be there, who will be the speakers, the companies, the associations present. Who do you want to talk to? What? What personal information can you find? The more prepared you are, the less nervous you'll be and the easier it will be to get the discussions going.

- **Be yourself** : don't try to play a character. If you're not comfortable in a suit, for example, don't force yourself! Be natural and authentic, this will prevent you from making mistakes and allow you to be more comfortable.

- **Listen more than you talk** : Prepare a few open-ended questions that you can use to spark discussions. Start a topic, then let your interlocutors do the talking. You take less risk, gain information to enrich the relationship, and leave a positive impression.

● **Have "cheat sheets"** : OK, you're not in college anymore, that's right. And yet, don't hesitate to prepare, on paper or on mobile, notes on the important points concerning this or that person or company. Take a look at it before approaching the person, you will be more confident and therefore more relevant!

Make the most of every opportunity

ALL FACE-TO-FACE NETWORKING opportunities are done over a set period of time. An evening for an afterwork, one or two days for a trade show or a conference, half a day for a breakfast debate... So, you need to make sure that every interaction counts and brings you closer to **your goals**, otherwise, it's just a waste of time.

Being ready is your number 1 mission. In addition to helping you be more comfortable, it will allow you to make every discussion more effective. But that's not all. Also, make sure you're "**memorable**."

The people you meet will also meet many other people, especially if it's a speaker or a representative of a company, for example.

Whether it's in the style (remember the example of the fuchsia sweater!) or in the business card you'll hand out after the discussion, make sure you ***stand out****.*

Also remember to follow the meetings you had during these events. For example, send an invitation on LinkedIn reminding you of the event you met or an email with a link to an article that provides additional information to the discussion you had.

Deliver value right away based on the exchanges you've had. You have a relatively short window of time after the event to quickly become a relationship of trust, seize it!

Offline networking is everywhere and all the time!

While professional events are great opportunities to network, keep in mind that they are not the only ones. In reality, and always because we are talking about human relationships, every moment is an opportunity to network.

Indeed, no matter what you do, you will have the opportunity to meet new **people**, and among them may be the contacts that will allow you to create new **opportunities** for yourself and meet your goals.

For example, if you go to the gym, or if you walk your dog always in the same neighborhood, always at the same times, there is a good chance that you will always meet the same people. You already have at least one relatively strong **point in common**, it's up to you to build a relationship that can potentially take you further, and why not, to your goals!

Start by **introducing** yourself, go to the other person to start the discussion. Get interested, ask **questions** and also be as **open** as possible about your job, your passions... The advantage is that you have time to build these relationships, as they are recurring encounters. Take this time, build over time.

In short

- Put your eggs in several baskets, also invest in face-to-face meetings. There's no substitute for a face-to-face relationship.

• Online and offline are complementary: speed and multiple opportunities on the one hand, proximity on the other. Combine the two and you'll find it easier to achieve your goals.

• Always be on the lookout for opportunities to meet people to start the relationship

Chapter XIV

Maintain your network over time

Networking is one thing. Nurturing it is another.

What do you do once you've achieved your main goals through your network? Or put your efforts into continuing to progress regardless, and how do you integrate your current and future network into that? Finally, how can we continue to **bring value** to all these people?

The biggest mistake is resting on your laurels. Once you've landed your dream job through your network, don't stop investing time and energy into it!

> *You probably don't know what else it has to offer you. Opportunities that you may never have thought of may be offered to you.*

For example, my main goal, working on my network, was to be able to work at LinkedIn. But while continuing to work on it, I was **recommended** by someone in my network that I didn't know very well to one of his contacts who was looking for a speaker for an international master's degree. This was not one of my objectives, just like OpenClassrooms for that matter, and yet, it is the efforts put in place to build my network and **maintain** it that allowed me to receive these proposals.

Get back on track

SO, ONCE YOU'VE ACHIEVED your goals, you're going to have to keep working. You may invest less time, be more strategic, but you'll still be **there**.

To start, you'll start at the beginning of this course and set new goals. Indeed, they are the ones who will guide your strategy and help you start a **new phase** of your networking.

New goals!

Also, try to **anticipate changes** that may take place in your network. Indeed, most of the time, it reflects a professional universe, market, profession, etc.

By anticipating innovations, upheavals, or simply their evolutions, you will remain the key contact to whom people turn to be informed and to progress in their profession. Your continuous **monitoring** should allow you to continue to bring value to your network and help it evolve.

Stay in touch

ONCE CONTACT IS MADE, interactions are made, a request is made, don't become a shadow member of your contact's network. Continue to send direct messages on a **regular basis.**

Share articles from your watch directly in their inbox, call them to check on them, offer to meet you at an event, tag them in a publication that you think is relevant to their current issues.

> *You will find it tempting **to let go** of relationships that have already "served" you, because they have acceded to your request and introduced you to the decision-maker you wanted to meet, for example. This is a **big mistake!***

Tell yourself that this was just the beginning of a relationship that it is up to you to enrich and evolve over time.

In short

- Creating and maintaining your network is a long-term exercise, but it also has benefits throughout your career.

- Don't wait until you need it to keep your network alive. You'll love giving to your connections and you'll receive a lot: job leads, career development, a new business.

Chapter XV

Get started and leverage your network!

It's up to you!

To practice, do this exercise step by step.

Now is the time to implement what you've learned throughout this course, and write two messages as part of your networking strategy. You can imagine the situation, but don't hesitate to take real situations so that it is useful to you!

Request for Connection

YOU WRITE THIS FIRST message to someone in your network to ask them to put you in touch with one of their connections that you would like to meet.

Direct request to a contact

THIS TIME, THERE IS no more intermediary, you write directly to someone in your network to ask them something. Information, advice, a request for mentorship, a meeting... Anything is possible, it's up to you to write a request that will make you want to respond!

Check your work

MAKE SURE YOU HAVE the following:

- The request for contact must be made with:

  ○ a relevant introduction;

  ○ clearly stated intentions;

  ○ an exit door for the contact to refuse;

  ○ a pre-written message.

- The direct request to a contact must be made with:

  ○ a title that makes you want to open it;

  ○ a clear goal;

  ○ a personal introduction;

  ○ key information that shows that the research has been carried out;

  ○ clear next steps;

  ○ Value delivered.

Have you completed the exercise? Congratulations! For my part, thank you for taking this course. I hope you found the inspiration you needed to build a quality network that will help you in your professional and even personal life!

Don't miss out!

Visit the website below and you can sign up to receive emails whenever Yves Guéchi publishes a new book. There's no charge and no obligation.

https://books2read.com/r/B-A-FPYDB-ETHXC

BOOKS 2 READ

Connecting independent readers to independent writers.

About the Author

Yves Guéchi, author and engineer, stands out for his remarkable contribution to sharing knowledge related to social networks and the use of the Internet in a professional context. His expertise, firmly anchored in the field, shines through his latest work, where he offers in-depth insight on how to take advantage of social networks to optimize your professional life.

As an engineer, Yves Guéchi brings a unique and innovative perspective to the intersection of technology and professional development, making him a key thought leader in his field. His passion for empowering individuals in the professional world is reflected not only in his writing, but also in his ongoing commitment to sharing innovative ideas and practical advice to help everyone reach their full potential in the digital age.